Survival!

DESERT

William B. Rice

Consultants

Timothy Rasinski, Ph.D.
Kent State University

Lori Oczkus
Literacy Consultant

Based on writing from
TIME For Kids. *TIME For Kids* and the *TIME For Kids* logo are registered trademarks of TIME Inc. Used under license.

Publishing Credits

Dona Herweck Rice, *Editor-in-Chief*
Lee Aucoin, *Creative Director*
Jamey Acosta, *Senior Editor*
Heidi Fiedler, *Editor*
Lexa Hoang, *Designer*
Stephanie Reid, *Photo Editor*
Rane Anderson, *Contributing Author*
Rachelle Cracchiolo, *M.S.Ed., Publisher*

Image Credits: p.22 Corbis; pp.17, 33 Getty Images; pp.18 (bottom), pp.20–21 (illustrations), pp.24, 27, 39 Timothy J. Bradley; pp.25 (top), 38 (bottom) iStockphoto; p.48 William Rice; All other images from Shutterstock.

Teacher Created Materials

5301 Oceanus Drive
Huntington Beach, CA 92649-1030
http://www.tcmpub.com
ISBN 978-1-4333-4818-1

TABLE OF CONTENTS

DESERTED!

The heat beats down from the sun like a weight. It presses on your head and shoulders. You are sleepy from the hot rays and so very thirsty. Licking your cracked lips, you wish you had packed a **canteen**. Your mouth and throat feel **parched** and dry as you swallow. Your skin is tight as you move. These are signs that your body is shutting down. You need water fast, but all you see is sand, the blazing sun, and prickly shrubs!

Lost and alone in the **desert**, seemingly far from help, you wonder how you got into this situation. And you need to know what you can do to survive.

About one-fifth of Earth's land is desert. These areas get very little rain or snow, and the air is very dry most of the year.

THINK LINK

- Find out the most important tool for desert survival.

- Discover how to conserve water and find food.

- Learn how to survive in the desert's extreme temperatures.

Deserts can be found on every continent.

It isn't common for people to be stranded in a desert, but it does happen. Maybe you are in a car driving through a desert, and the car breaks down. Maybe you are hiking in a desert and become lost. Or maybe you are the victim of **foul play**!

When traveling through, to, or near a desert, a smart person goes prepared—just in case.

Whenever you travel, it is always a good idea to be prepared for emergencies.

Emergency!

flare gun

reflective blanket

Planning for desert survival starts at home. Take emergency supplies with you. Better safe than sorry! Supplies should include an emergency kit. Such kits usually include basic medical supplies, **flares**, and **reflectors**. These are some of the most important items to include in your kit.

tools for building a shelter

clothes for warmth

water to last you several days

Deserts Around the World

No two deserts are exactly alike. What is most threatening in one desert may not be a threat in another. A key to your survival is preparation.

Syrian Desert

Dust storms occur in deserts around the world. Sometimes they come on so quickly, there isn't time to find shelter. The dust can blind travelers. In some cases, a dust storm can lift over a mile into the air.

Namib Desert

Morning fog is something we usually see near water. The Namib Desert is special. Cold ocean currents and strong winds form dense clouds of fog. They drift inland over the desert. The moisture in the fog helps some species survive. How would you use it to survive in the desert?

Gobi Desert

Traveling on foot across a desert can be dangerous! But every year, trained athletes gather for the Gobi March. It's a 155-mile **trek** across one of the harshest deserts in the world. Some athletes collapse during the race from **heat exhaustion.**

The Australian Outback

The Australian Outback is home to some of the world's deadliest snakes and spiders. One bite could send you to your grave. But when treated by a doctor, most bites aren't deadly.

ATTITUDE IS EVERYTHING!

At some point, of course, you realize you're stranded. Either you are lost or your vehicle has broken down and you cannot get it going.

Whatever your situation, **attitude** and clear thinking are the most important tools for survival. *Let's say that again.* Attitude and clear thinking are the most important tools for survival. Got it?

Panic and emotions can cloud the mind and lead to poor and possibly deadly decisions. You and your wonderful brain are the main tools that will help you survive. Your attitude and your response to your situation will affect your outcome. You must stay calm to think clearly.

Spend time making a detailed plan for your survival. Never rush into a decision. Stop. Think. Act.

Don't panic! Take long, deep breaths to calm down. Slowly inhale while you count to ten. Then exhale while you count to 10.

PLANNING TO SURVIVE!

Deserts are places of extremes. **Exposure** to these extremes can have severe effects on the human body. Taking care of your body must be your main focus.

Deserts are dry places. So, you must choose your actions with care to make sure you don't get **dehydrated** (dee-HAHY-drey-ted). Deserts can get very hot during the day. But as the sun sets, the desert can grow very cold. Take extra care to be sure you do not overheat or get too cold.

Before you do anything else, address your immediate situation. Consider the air temperature. If it is hot, get to a shady place. Look for a spot under a tree or on the shady side of a large boulder or a rocky ledge. If it is cold, find a way to stay warm. Put on extra clothes, build a fire, or cover yourself with a blanket. It may be best to stay inside your car with the windows and doors closed.

Why So Extreme?

Why do desert temperatures cover such extremes? The lack of clouds, rain, and plant life all work together to create very high and very low temperatures.

Desert heat can rise above 120°F during the day!

TAKING STOCK

Once you have taken care of your immediate needs, think about your overall situation. Then, make a plan for surviving and getting help.

What season is it? What time of day? In the winter, the desert can get very cold at night—even below freezing. In the summer, it can get extremely hot during the day. Stop to think about these things. These factors should affect your choices about when and how to take action. For example, during the winter, when it is very cold at night, it is best to travel during the day. During the summer months, when it's very hot, it's best to move at night.

If you are stranded in a group, make sure to travel at the pace of the slowest person. That way, you won't lose anyone.

The ABCs of Survival

An Australian survivalist named Bob Cooper teaches the ABCs of survival. He says there are five key things to do to get in the right frame of mind and survive.

- **A**ccept your situation.
  (Stop wishing things were different!)
- **B**rew a cup of tea.
  (That means to pause a moment to think.)
- **C**onsider your options.
- **D**ecide on a plan.
- **E**xecute the plan.

Do not sit in your car during the day waiting for help. It will be hotter than inside an oven. Instead, sit in the shade your car creates.

People of the Desert

People have been living in deserts for thousands of years. Their strength and skill may inspire you as you make a plan for desert survival.

San Bushmen of Southern Africa

The San Bushmen are excellent hunters. Their bows and arrows take down animals as small as an antelope and as large as a giraffe. They smear poison made from the larvae of a beetle onto their arrows. The poison does not kill the animal right away. Sometimes, the San Bushmen must track the animal for days before it dies.

Bedouin of the Middle East

Long ago, the Bedouin (BED-oo-in) used woven goat hair to make their shelters. Their tents not only protected them from the rain but also kept them cool during the summer heat. Today, their tents are made from more modern materials.

Aborigines of Australia

Aborigines (ab-uh-RIJ-uh-nees) are experts when it comes to finding water. They have survived in the Outback for thousands of years. They follow animal tracks to water holes. They collect water from trees and roots. They even squeeze water out of frogs.

Shoshone and Cahuilla of North America

Native American tribes, such as the Shoshone (shoh-SHOH-nee) and the Cahuilla (kuh-WEE-uh) of the Mojave desert, use plants to heal common illnesses. Cacti heal cuts and wounds, while other plants ease pain and sickness.

Gulp!

To survive in the desert, you need to drink about half a gallon of water each day. The more active you are, the more you need.

A lean-to is a shelter made especially for shade and protection from the elements.

You will also want to think about the resources you have on hand. What do you have? The most important resource is water. How much do you have? Also, look around. Do you have the means to make a shelter? What can you use that will help? Look for a group of rocks or tall shrubs that will block out the sun. And do you have a map? How far are you from help? Carefully climb the tallest object nearby to scan your surroundings. Do you see a road or a town in the distance? You'll need all this information to make a plan.

Look Around!

Resources are not limited to what you brought with you. Look around to see what you can find in nature. Trees, plants, rocks, and more are part of your available supplies.

DIG DEEPER!

Survival Showdown!

You are stranded in the middle of the Sahara desert. All your survival gear is about to be lost forever in a massive sandstorm headed your way. You only have time to grab a few supplies. Which ones will you take?

Food **or** Water

Food

Food gives you energy.

but

You can't digest food without water.

Water

You need to drink half a gallon a day in the desert.

but

It won't calm your hunger.

Whistle **or** Mirror

Whistle

You can sound the alarm and call for help.

but

In the desert, there might not be anyone to hear you.

Mirror

You can send a signal a great distance.

but

It won't help in the dark of night.

Axe

or

Knife

It cuts through strong materials, such as trees and coconuts.

but

It adds weight to your pack.

It's easy to carry.

but

It can only cut thin or weak things, such as snakes and grass.

Compass

or

Flashlight

This may be just what you need to find your way home.

but

It doesn't do much else!

You'll be able to see at night.

but

Who wants to see a scorpion?

MAKING A PLAN

Once you know what you have and what your conditions are, you can make a plan. It's very important to do this. Stranded in the desert, any action taken without careful thought can have deadly **consequences**.

Your plan should focus on taking care of your body first and then finding a way to get help. It may take a little time to find help or for help to find you. So, make a step-by-step plan that includes all the ways you can protect yourself. Think about water, shelter, food, and help. Make a plan for all these things.

In making your decision to get help, you really have two options. One option is to stay put and wait for help to come to you. The other option is to walk to find help.

Beat the Heat

Maybe help is just a few miles away. But if it's the middle of the day and blazing hot, walking even a short distance can be deadly. That's why you need a plan. Get shelter and then walk only when it's cool and safe.

127 Hours

The movie *127 Hours* is the true story of a man who fell off a cliff in the desert and got trapped with his arm stuck under a boulder. Aron Ralston had only what was in his backpack to survive and no way to get help. He made the decision to cut off his arm. He was in extreme pain, but he kept thinking and planning. He never gave up. Although he had to take extreme measures, he survived to tell his story. He continues to climb mountains today.

FINDING WHAT YOU NEED!

If you have prepared and kept your **wits** about you, you may have everything you need to survive. But if you don't, there are ways to get what you need.

WATER

You need water, and plenty of it, to stay alive. In the heat, your body loses water through **perspiration**. You also lose water as you breathe. Have you ever noticed the fog your breath makes on a cold day? That is a visible sign of the water **vapor** you lose with every breath.

Don't panic. The truth is you have options for getting water even though it seems dry everywhere you look. Do not **ration** your water. Instead, listen to your body. It is better to keep the water inside you than in a container. Also, be still during the hottest times of day. You are always sweating. The more you move, the more you sweat, and the more water your body loses. By the time you feel thirsty, your body is already dehydrated.

When you exhale, you breath out water vapor.

24

Hydration Pack

A hydration pack is a special backpack with a plastic bag inside it. The bag is connected to a long tube. A hiker can carry a lot of water in the pack and use the tube to drink water throughout the day.

A person needs to drink two quarts of water per day to stay alive in the desert.

You may not see it, but water is available in the desert. You just have to know where to look and how to gather it. Find the edge of a dry **streambed**. Once you locate it, dig down. There is a good chance you will find water. You can also build a **solar still** to capture water.

Building a Solar Still

1. During cooler moments in the day, dig a hole about three feet around and two feet deep. Look for an area with sun and damp dirt.

2. In the middle of the hole, dig a smaller, deeper hole.

3. Place a container such as a can in the small hole.

4. Stretch a plastic sheet across the big hole. Secure the edges with stones or sand. Make sure the plastic is not touching the bottom or sides of the hole.

5. Place a small stone in the middle of the plastic sheet just above the container. Now, the middle of the plastic sheet points down.

6. As water rises from the soil, it will condense on the bottom of the plastic. Slowly, it will drain into the container for you to drink. Add a rubber or vinyl drinking tube so water can be sipped as it collects.

condensation

evaporation

drinking

PROTECTION

One of the biggest dangers in the desert is exposure to extreme temperatures. During extreme cold, extra layers of clothing and blankets are very important. During extreme heat, you need loose, light clothing that covers your body. This includes a hat, long sleeves, and long pants or a long skirt. Think about the people who live in deserts around the world. The clothing they wear protects their skin from the sun. It also traps moisture near their bodies.

Shelter also offers a very important form of protection. Remember the lean-to? If you can't find natural shelter, building a shelter is essential.

Weather Watch

Keep an eye out for storm clouds. In the desert, storms can affect large areas, even those far away. **Flash floods** happen suddenly in the desert. These floods are powerful and can sweep away everything in their paths.

WARNING!
Flash Flood Area

Animal **Attack**

Watch for creatures of all shapes and sizes. Snakes, **scorpions**, and spiders are some common desert animals. A bite or sting can seriously injure or kill a person— especially if far from help.

Light and loose-fitting clothes help keep desert travelers cool.

Animals of the Desert

Every desert is home to unique animals that have adapted to survive the harsh elements. Humans can look to these animals for clues on how to stay alive in the desert.

Black Vultures

Many desert animals are pale in color. This allows their bodies to reflect heat rather than absorb it. Black vultures may attract the heat, but they have adapted to stay cool. They urinate on their legs. As they dry, they cool off. A person can soak an extra shirt in water and wrap it around his or her head to lower body temperature.

Night Creatures

Some animals are only active at dawn or nighttime, when temperatures are coolest. It is an adaptation that helps them keep cool and use less water. Humans can also rest during the day in a cool, shady area and move around at night.

STOP! THINK...

- How do animals survive in the desert?

- What clues can you learn from animals about staying cool?

- What clues can you learn from animals about where to find water in the desert?

Namib Desert Beetle

The Namib desert beetle collects water from the morning fog. Humans can lick dew from plant leaves.

FOOD

Food only becomes an issue if you are stranded for a while. A person can survive three or four weeks without eating. But you can only survive a couple days without water. If you have food but not much water, don't eat! It takes a lot of water to digest food.

If you don't have food, you may be able to find some. Some cacti are good food sources. But don't eat anything bitter. A strong bitter taste may be a sign the food is not good for you. Plants with milky sap are probably harmful, too, so don't eat them, either. Most bugs can be eaten. Worms, grasshoppers, crickets, and ants are best.

How to Eat Barrel Cactus

Cut off the top of the cactus and scoop out the inside. Squeeze the water from it into your mouth. Then, you can eat the cactus **pulp**.

How to Eat Prickly Pear

Cut off a piece of the prickly pear and roast it over a fire to burn off the thorns. Then, peel off the outer skin and eat the inside. Those who have eaten it say it is quite tasty!

You can eat most kinds of lizards. But you probably shouldn't eat a Gila (HEE-luh) monster—it's venomous.

DIG DEEPER!

Plants in the Desert

Much like desert animals, plants have adapted to survive in the dry climate. Humans can look to these plants for ways to stay alive in the desert.

Perennials

Some plants are **dormant** through the desert's driest times of the year. But when there is more water, they come back to life. It's important to rest during the day if you're lost in the desert. This will allow you to use your energy at night, when it's cooler.

Taproots

Phreatophytes (free-AT-uh-fahyts) are plants with roots that poke into the earth like long straws. These long, skinny roots are called *taproots*. The taproots help plants get water from deep in the earth. Some taproots grow as long as 20 feet deep. Humans should follow the taproots, and dig deep to find water.

The Gobi's Superstar

The saxaul (SAK-sol) tree is an important plant in the Gobi desert. It stores water for dry times. Animals and humans can press water from the tree's bark by chewing it.

GETTING HELP!

Next to survival, the most important thing is to get help. You must decide whether to walk for help or wait for help to come to you. It may be best to stay put, especially if people are expecting you. When you don't show up, they will probably come looking for you.

If you choose to walk for help, be very sure you know where the help is. Otherwise, you could be walking into a situation that's even worse. Also, walk only during cool times of the day. You may need to shorten your journey into several parts over several days to save your strength and water or to rest and stock up again.

Be aware and keep your eyes open. Watch out for cliffs, steep rocky slopes, and other dangers.

Watch for signs of heat exhaustion, such as feeling dizzy, nauseated, and sweaty. Headaches can also be a sign of heat exhaustion.

GETTING NOTICED

If you stay put and wait for help, you will want to make it easy for people to find you. You can build a fire and make lots of smoke. Or try using a signal mirror to attract attention. A loud whistle can be heard at great distances. You can also set out a bright cloth so airplanes can see you from above. It may be a good idea to build a large **SOS** message.

How to Signal

Rescuers may search from above in an airplane, but they may not be able to see you. If you shine a light toward the sky, they may be able to see that.

Step 1

To signal with a mirror, raise it in front of your face with the reflecting side out. Stretch out your other hand and form a *V* with your thumb and fingers.

Step 2

Move the mirror so you can "capture" the sun's reflection in the *V* of your extended hand.

Step 3

Keep the light in the *V* until the plane is also in the *V*. Now the reflected light will be pointed directly at the plane. Move the mirror slightly to make the signal flash.

Warning: do not do this unless there is an emergency. You should never flash lights at planes for fun.

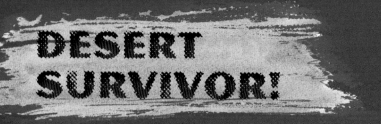

DESERT SURVIVOR!

No one wants to be stranded in the desert. It's uncomfortable at best and deadly at worst, but you *can* survive. Even if you are not prepared, the desert can give you what you need if you stay calm and make a plan.

The most important thing is having a good attitude! Believing that you can survive is the key to actually surviving. Your attitude keeps you going. It keeps you thinking. And it can make you a desert survivor!

How Would You Survive?

- If you were lost in the desert, what would you look for first? Food? Shelter? Water? Help?

- What tools would you want with you if you were lost?

- Would you rather be lost in the desert during the day or at night? Why?

GLOSSARY

attitude—a manner, position, or feeling about something

canteen—a small container for carrying liquids

consequences—effects, outcomes, or results of actions taken

dehydrated—deprived of water

desert—a dry area of land with very little rainfall and little plant life

dormant—not active, but capable of becoming active; appearing to be asleep

exposure—the state of being without shelter or protection from elements such as sun and wind

flares—fire or light used to signal

flash floods—sudden rushes of water, usually caused by heavy rain

foul play—criminal action or intentional harm to another person

heat exhaustion—a condition marked by weakness, nausea, dizziness, and sweating resulting from a hot environment

parched—scorched and dry

perspiration—moisture given off so the body can cool itself

pulp—the soft, juicy part inside a fruit or plant

ration—to restrict the amount being used

reflectors—polished surfaces made to reflect, or throw back, light

scorpion—an invertebrate that has a long jointed body and a slender tail with a poisonous stinger at the end

solar still—a device for collecting water

SOS—a call for help, a signal understood internationally

streambed—a channel in which a stream flows

trek—to travel a great distance

wits—mental stability and senses

vapor—the gas form of a liquid; one of three states of matter, the other two being solid and liquid

INDEX

BIBLIOGRAPHY

Arnosky, Jim. *Watching Desert Wildlife.* **National Geographic Society, 2002.**

This National Geographic Society book contains detailed illustrations and information on a variety of desert wildlife, including Gila monsters, birds of prey, and bighorn sheep.

Hodge, Deborah. *Who Lives Here? Desert Animals.* **Kids Can Press, 2008.**

Even though the desert has a tough climate, many animals have adapted to live there. This book tells about these animals and includes colorful illustrations.

Long, Denise. *Survivor Kid: A Practical Guide to Wilderness Survival.* **Chicago Review Press, 2011.**

This book explains a variety of survival skills and techniques for kids, including how to build a shelter, important navigation skills, and how to stay safe if you encounter wild animals.

National Geographic Society. *Creatures of the Desert World.* **National Geographic Children's Books, 1991.**

This National Geographic Society book contains detailed and interactive illustrations with information on different animals and their desert habitats.

Serafini, Frank. *Looking Closely Across the Desert.* **Kids Can Press, 2008.**

This book shows images of the desert from a close-up perspective. Photographs of plants, animals, and landscapes give a unique picture of desert life.

Blue Planet Biomes
http://www.blueplanetbiomes.org/desert.htm

Blue Planet Biomes gives information on different biomes around the world. Students can learn more about the climate, plants, and animals found in the world's most famous deserts.

Inch in a Pinch
http://inchinapinch.com/

On the left, click on *Deserts*. This website has photos and descriptions of many deserts. Below that, there are two buttons that lead you to even more photos and information about desert plants and animals.

National Geographic for Kids
http://kids.nationalgeographic.com/kids/

National Geographic's website for kids provides information on animals and photos and videos of wildlife from around the world, as well as games and other activities.

Encyclopedia Britannica for Kids
http://kids.britannica.com/

Encyclopedia Britannica Online provides kids with a searchable database of information on any content you are studying in class. Encyclopedia entries are written for kids ages 8–11 or 11 and up.

Survival Zone
http://www.yourdiscovery.com/survival_zone

This website has survival tips and techniques for the desert, ocean, and tropics. It also has suggestions for handling other worst-case scenarios.

ABOUT THE AUTHOR

William B. Rice grew up in Pomona, California, and graduated from Idaho State University with a degree in geology. He works at a California state agency that strives to protect the quality of surface and groundwater resources. Protecting and preserving the environment is important to him, and he works to protect deserts and other natural areas around the world. He is married with two children and lives in Southern California.